The Robin Book

by Jane Russ

GRAFFEG

Dedication

To the memory of my mother Ruth,
who loved robins best above all
other birds.

Contents

5   Introduction

9   Physiology of the Robin

31   Timeline

72   Leucistic Robins

75   Migration

83   Tales from the Robin's Nest

93   British Trust for Ornithology

99   The Robin in Myth and Legend

115   The Robin in Art and Literature

156   Photo credits

158   Acknowledgements

Introduction

My starting point for this book was the seminal work about robins, *The Life of the Robin* by David Lack.

First published to much acclaim in 1943, it remains *the* most comprehensive, influential and accessible work about this most beloved of British birds. Written for the amateur ornithologist, the book is very readable and Lack pulls you in with details of behaviour which are both fascinating and, in some cases, unexpected.

Much to my surprise, I discovered that I had a personal link to Lack's work on the robin, as it had been written between 1933 and 1939 whilst he was a biology teacher at Dartington Hall School. I attended the same school in South Devon in the late 60s and early 70s. I know the

area of copse where he studied his birds very well indeed, walking past it every day on my way to the school building just beyond. Suddenly, Lack's robins were my robins too.

There are many, many tales of robins making connections with humans over the death of loved ones or seemingly appearing to offer support in times of stress. I think this ability to connect with us is what makes them so special. In 1960 *The Times* ran a poll to find out which was considered to be our national bird: perhaps unsurprisingly, the robin won. It was still top in 2015, when BBC *Springwatch* presenter and ornithologist David Lindo asked the question again. This time the robin gained the support of 34% of the 224,000 people who voted online, the barn owl coming second with a mere 12%.

Naturally I hope you will find this book a 'good read'. Perhaps more importantly, however, it will give you an insight into the life and times of this great British ornithological treasure.

Physiology of the Robin

Physiology of the Robin

The robin has had many names; originally known as the ruddock, then robin redbreast and finally just robin. It does of course have a full family, genus and Latin name, although like many birds, there are still issues outstanding in relation to its genus connections to other birds. Initially, along with chats, it was thought to be a small thrush-type bird – like redstarts and stonechats, of the genus *Turdidae*. This genus contained birds of the thrush-type and the smaller birds sat in this group for no other reason than they were quality singers who moved with a somewhat springy, lively hop. DNA sequencing however, proved them to be quite different from thrushes and, in subsequent investigations, even from each other. It would seem it is possible that the robin may yet be in a genus of one. Research continues.

Family *Muscicapidae*
Subfamily *Saxicolinae* (chats)
Genus *Erithacus*
Species *E. rubecula*
Latin Name *Erithacus rubecula*
Length 14cm
Wing span Approx. 20-22cm
Weight 14-21g

The look of the robin is so well known in the English landscape that it seems laboured to describe it here. Suffice to say that the adult male and female look identical. Young birds have a sort of overall golden spot to their rich brown colouring, rather than a red breast.

The body of a robin has a layer of smooth top feathers and a down layer underneath for warmth. Their legs are long, strong and without feathers but if cold, they can be folded at the 'hocks' into a

Juvenile robin

hunkered-down position and covered with the body feathers. Like many birds, robins have four widely-spreading toes, three pointing forward and one pointing backwards, making for maximum grip on the branch and steadiness on the ground.

Robins are very 'non-specific' about food and great opportunists as anyone who has dug over a border or veg patch will agree. Feeding mainly on the ground on insects, they are also keen bird table users and can even just about manage to hang onto a nut feeder more often frequented by blue tits and great tits. Ever the versatile feeder, they can catch slow insects in flight like a flycatcher, pull worms like a thrush and grip onto a tree trunk and forage like a tree creeper.

An interesting and little-known fact about robins is that if they eat something indigestible like a hard part of an insect or seed, they will eject it in pellet form, just like a bird of prey. Naturally if there are no hard parts there will be no pellets.

It can be seen from any of the pictures in this book that robin's eyes are large comparative to their size. This means they get as much light as possible into the eye, which in its turn means they can see clearly to feed in low light conditions; before dawn, after dusk and in shadowed areas under hedges. Their hearing is quite acute too, which is useful for listening for other robins in

They will of course augment anything to be found in the 'wild' with foodstuffs offered on a bird table and very much consider it as 'their table', seeing off other birds if necessary.

their territory and for detecting prey rustling in the grass. The turning of the seasons will naturally play a part in the available diet for the robin, more insects and invertebrates in spring and summer and more seeds and berries in autumn and winter. This makes sense for a small bird like the robin as seeds have a high fat content and will help see them through any cold snaps the British weather might offer up. They will of course augment anything to be found in the 'wild' with foodstuffs offered on a bird table and very much consider it as 'their table', seeing off other birds if necessary.

One great joy of the robin is that it sings almost all year round. There is a 'spring song', starting just before

the turn of the year until mid-June. This is followed by a slightly diluted-sounding 'autumn song' from mid-July as youngsters join in, until late December when the spring song takes over again. Rather like humans, there are good singers and those that are not so good. Females sing as well as males, particularly through the autumn but they will usually stop in the spring when they have found a mate. Robins have been recorded singing next to street lights at night. Singing does of course have another function, to mark the territory of the bird, and we shall go into this in depth a little later. The importance of learning the song from your own species is important too. The song of adult male robins

is marked by an increase in volume when the young are fledged. Experiments have shown that the robin's song is learnt, not instinctive. Therefore this strengthening of the song just when the youngsters are going out into the world is imprinting it on them for future use.

We don't trap the robin in this country any more but in the past it was trapped as a cage bird, hence William Blake's famous lines from *Auguries of Innocence* (1863), "a robin redbreast in a cage, puts all heaven in a rage." On the continent in past centuries, the bird was cooked and sold in markets, although one does wonder how many you would need to make a reasonable meal. David Lack in *The Life of the Robin* explains that the robin is so easy to trap, that he never had to wait longer than two hours to attract a captive and often it would only take two minutes. Amusingly, he had one bird that was trapped seven times on one day and eight on the next, it sat and waited for him to leave the trap before hopping in again. It never learned how to escape.

This ease of trapping is perhaps the most important reason that Lack was able to work so cleanly through his recording of the life of robins in his twenty-acre study copse in Devon. Each robin was colour-ringed with up to three colours so that at any point observations were always on a specific robin. Individual behaviour could be noted and compared with that of others and fights and alliances between the sexes taken into account.

Timeline

Timeline

The timeline of the robin has to start with the annual moult in July/August. It sets the birds up for their year and each cock will then begin looking for a territory. Hens hold territories too but not always and the rest that don't will migrate. All inhabitants of an area will be singing, posturing and fighting through the autumn, with songs and 'attitude' getting weaker towards the end of the year.

In late December/early January, the song of the male will revive and he will hopefully pair up with a female. It may be a female with an adjacent territory or an outsider who has migrated back. From December to early March, the cock and hen will share the space.

From mid-March onwards there will be the usual round of courtship, nest-building, mating, egg laying and feeding. There may be more than one clutch in a season, after which both the birds will retire to quietude and prepare for the moult.

This timeline can vary based on geographical position in the country. Northern birds may run just behind birds in the slightly warmer south. Individuals can vary too, even within the same area.

The moult

During an active year feathers, which are an outstanding example of design and engineering being both light and strong, get damaged and need replacing. Birds can fall prey to lice or feather mites despite their best preening efforts. Preening is an important grooming technique to all birds; lining up all the barbs on their feathers. These barbs fit together rather like velcro, gripping

Juvenile beginning to lose
its spotted plumage.

Robin with feather mites.

Robins will bathe in water, and seem to relish it.

onto each other and when smoothed with a beak the 'fit' is restored. Preen oil (from a gland near the tail) is smoothed over the feathers, thus making them waterproof and smooth for flight. Head and face feathers are worked on with the foot brought over the wing to scratch at the required area.

Robins will bathe in water, and seem to relish it. Another cleansing process that robins and several hundred other birds use is anting, where they will lie down and 'bathe' near an ant colony with wings outstretched and feathers fluffed. The ants crawl over the birds, squirting their secretions, which include formic acid. It is not proven but has been suggested that formic acid acts as a kind of insecticide or perhaps it's just a way for the robin to eat acid-free ants as they will pick the insects off afterwards. Other insects such as millipedes are used by some birds in the anting and it is possible the whole process is linked to moulting but this is unproven. It may just be that ants are more active in the summer.

Coming as it does after the stresses of breeding, the moult ensures that the bird begins the year with the best feathers available to keep it waterproof and warm through the winter. The moult takes several weeks and robins show no aggression during this period. In late July, when the juveniles begin to lose their spotted plumage, they start to sing and by the time the red breast comes in they will also be 'test fighting' but in rather a perfunctory manner: a perceived interloper might be harried one minute and left alone the next.

By early August adults who are moulting might start to sing and chase. Within a couple of weeks each will have carved out a specific fresh territory, with some hens being just as fierce as cocks. The juveniles, who were keen to fight in early autumn, are much quieter by October as the territorial boundaries of older birds become arranged around them. Trespass still happens of course but juveniles will try to be more unobtrusive. Adults will occasionally attack trespassing juveniles but never their own offspring. Once the youngsters are in full plumage however, there is no recognition of family members and it becomes all about ownership. Every adolescent is now a potential interloper in the territorial game that is the life of the robin.

Marking the territory with song

A robin's day is made up of singing and fighting. Singing is a way of marking territory and robins sing the equivalent of "...you lookin' at me?" at neighbours but will not venture over the neighbour's boundary if they are present. Two cocks on adjoining plots will sing at each other very vigorously and strike an attitude which leaves no doubt about their intentions. This aggressive territorial marking, combined with a cross, beady expression, gives the lie to the chintzy robin look we have come to expect at Christmas. Robins have a constant drive to mark what is theirs. Perhaps surprisingly, they do in fact venture across borders in search of food and Lack's observations in Devon back this up. Quality of food is a draw that is worth the risk of

reprisals and birds will keep a low profile to get at a good food source 'owned' by another robin.

An ideal territory should contain a good food source, a choice of secure places for nesting, water for drinking and bathing and not be so large that it is too hard to defend. Quality beats size in a perfect location choice.

To a robin, territory is everything. When the owner of an area has been posturing and loud singing, intruder birds will usually retire, often closely chased by the incumbent. It may seem hard to understand how the robins know they have a territory at all. They do however behave quite differently inside and outside their own region.

Inside their territory	Outside their territory
they sing, loudly and often	they do not sing
they fight	they do not fight
they display	they do not display
they are conspicuous	they make themselves inconspicuous
they patrol the space	they return to their territory

If the individual dies and their space becomes vacant, it may be taken by the expansion of a neighbour or a completely new bird, perhaps a youngster just waiting for a chance to step into a vacant area. It only takes about forty-eight hours after

arrival for a new bird to map out their territory and confirm the boundaries, as any neighbour will make it plain what is theirs. The defending of boundaries is on-going but interestingly, although there will be posturing, loud singing and chasing, there is almost never any actually fighting between neighbours. Fighting only occurs as a last resort. If an interloper is testing to see whether an area is owned by another robin, it will start low down in the bushes, singing quietly. Only when it meets with no resistance will it take to the treetops and sing out its ownership. Wing to wing fighting seems to be quite rare and merely chasing and loud, quality singing appears to be enough to hold the territory. When locked in a fight however, the two birds are completely absorbed. I have personal experience of a ball of fighting robins falling at my feet and paying no attention to me at all. I walked away and left them to it but a predator might not and serious fighting makes both combatants very vulnerable. If a 'won' territory has a female already attached, then the victor will usually take her on as his partner as well. Of course, all of the above presupposes relatively good weather conditions. In a hard winter, robins will not waste precious energy on marking their boundaries; hostilities will be suspended for the duration.

The red breast of the robin is the strongest fight signal and many well-documented experiments (including ones by David Lack) have been carried out to demonstrate this fact. An adult robin will even attack a small bundle of red feathers, something which can pose

absolutely no threat whatsoever to the live bird. What is perhaps most surprising is that, on such occasions, responses can vary enormously from full-blown posturing with shouting and finally attacking to just mild posturing. Robins vary in their attitude to a threat. Furthermore, if the 'threat' is presented to the live robin on more than one occasion, with each presentation the response diminishes; excepting in the case of an unusually aggressive robin.

Robins are not just pugnacious with their own, they will attack other birds who are on 'their feeder' or any other area they consider to be theirs.

Pairing off

By mid-December the females will leave their own territories and pair up with a male. The female selects the male, not the other way around. The chosen one may be from a neighbouring territory but not necessarily. He will posture and sing at her aggressively but she, instead of backing off, will fly up to him. The action is repeated perhaps several times and the hen may sing back at the cock but, more importantly, she does not back off. It is this not backing down which seems to trigger an understanding that she is not an aggressor and he will then follow her around, singing quietly. It is estimated that each year one fifth of cocks do not gain a mate. A male may have no mate one year and acquire one the next so it does not mean they will never have a mate.

Having paired off, the couple now hold a territory jointly and ownership of this will only change if the female abandons him or a fight is lost with an interloper.

In the latter case it can take a couple of hours for the victorious male to realise that he should not chase off his newly acquired mate, he will need time to adjust to not 'seeing off' this particular intruder. Pairs normally stay together but it is well documented that cocks can be deserted, either during the betrothal period or even between broods. Bigamy amongst robins has also been witnessed with one male supporting two broods.

This diagram (right) illustrates the shifting ownership of a small area of David Lack's study copse and one can imagine it being reproduced throughout the country.

In October, when the examination of this area started, this is how the territories fell and these were all new birds to the study. All sang well except B, who was never heard to sing.

In December, C (a cock) came into song, took over the territory of D and paired up with F (a hen) so they now shared this ground together.

Towards the end of January, A, who had sung well since October, disclosed herself to be a hen and she moved across the copse to join up with E (a cock). B also revealed as a hen and moved to the next copse and out of the study area. The vacuum left by these two departures was soon filled by cock G, who was new, and C and F appropriated B's corner to enlarge their patch even further.

Subsequently, E was killed by a cat and A moved back to her original corner and paired up with G.

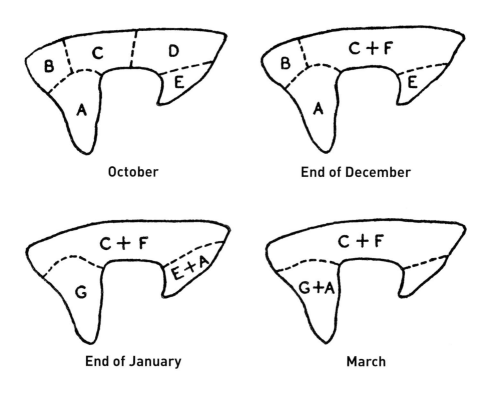

October

End of December

End of January

March

IMPORTANT
DEPRESS CLUTCH WHEN
OPERATING OVERDRIVE
PERIODICALL CHECK
OVERDRIVE O L LEVEL

Nest building, courtship and mating

After the pairing off, a long period of 'betrothal' ensues and the male and female rub along together, sharing their territory. The nest is generally built around March but there are documented occurrences both well before and well after this, although survival of chicks under early and late nesting conditions can be challenging.

Only the female builds the nest and she will often do it in shifts over several days. It comprises a soft cup with a moss/dead leaf foundation lined with grasses, feathers and any other soft materials available. (Dog owners often comb their dogs outside to allow birds to pick over the soft combings.) Robins have a reputation for building nests in some pretty unlikely places. These two pictures certainly seem to prove this in a big way!

The hen robin only ever sees the

courtship of her chosen male prior to mating. Courtship is not done to 'win' the female as it is in many bird species; she has already chosen her mate long before any courtship begins. Courtship consists of the female calling softly, fluttering her wings and dipping to the male in a begging posture, almost as though she were a chick. Food is accepted from him and during this period she may source no food for herself but sit and wait for a tasty morsel from the ever-attentive male. Not only does this courtship ensure that the hen is well fed and in top condition for egg laying but she could leave

Courtship ensures that the hen is well fed and in top condition for egg laying.

and find another mate if she felt his provisions were not going to be up to standard for any young she might produce. Mating usually occurs soon after the courtship feeding ends.

The eggs are laid several days after mating, often in the morning, and the hen will lay one each day until the clutch is complete. A brood can be anything from four to seven eggs, with five or six being normal. Larger clutches are found in birds the further north one goes; the shortness of the summers there meaning there are probably only two sets a year as opposed to three in the slightly warmer south. The eggs are a rich cream with a slight blush of cinnamon. Confusingly, it is the American robin's egg that lends its name to the colour 'robin's egg blue'.

Incubation takes thirteen to fourteen days and does not begin until all the eggs are laid: consequently the eggs will all hatch at once. The hen will not leave the nest during the incubation period but will be fed by the cock; he takes no part in actually sitting on the eggs. It is to be expected that during incubation all thoughts of defence are forgotten, however, the male will call and warn of any impending danger. Once the eggs are hatched, the female defends the nest area with vigour.

To begin with the female will sit on the nest and keep the blind and nearly bald chicks safe and warm. By the end of their second week after hatching, they are feathered enough to be left whilst the hen and the cock gather food. Softer insects and larvae are the primary nourishment initially, but soon the tireless robin parents are bringing an estimated 1,000 items a

day to their insatiable brood. Not only do they provide sustenance but they also remove the waste that the chicks produce. The chicks helpfully raise their bottoms up to the parent, who carries the semi-solid lump away to be dropped elsewhere, thus ensuring that the nest remains well hidden to predators.

At fourteen days old the chicks will fledge, although they won't fly well as they have shorter tail and wing feathers than they will have in their adult form. Their initial plumage does not have a red breast but is a rich chestnut brown all over, with little spots of a golden honey colour at the tip of each feather. Once they have left the nest, the chicks will beg for food from the parents...and any other passing robin. They will even try another species, I have seen a chick begging a great tit for food.

The great tit was unimpressed.

Chicks will follow the adult and wait to be fed but eventually they begin to take an interest in what is happening and will join in. Independence lies ahead. The male will probably continue the feeding alone for the final couple of weeks before the chicks moult and fully fledge as the female prepares the nest for the next brood.

Two or three clutches later, once breeding is completely over, the hen may find an adjacent territory or move further away. There is no love lost between former spouses and the cock will see her off his patch as fiercely as he might any other intruder. A cock and hen may mate again in a subsequent season but it is the territory that is the draw rather than the former mate.

Leucistic Robins

If you see a bird that is obviously, by its stance, a robin but it has some white feathers, this bird is probably leucistic. The only difference between it and an albino bird is the eye colour. Albinos always have a red eye, whereas any other bird with an issue resulting in white feathers has a normal eye for that bird.

Melanin, the important pigment that is missing in leucistic birds, is absent through an inherited gene malformation. It can also result in weaker feathers that might inhibit flight, making any birds not only more conspicuous but therefore more open to predation. The positioning of the white feathers varies and is not inherited. If the gene is recessive it can also skip a generation.

Migration

Migration

Perhaps the most obvious and well-known bird migrants to the UK are swallows and swifts. Their return to previous nest sites across the country often elicits great excitement in local humans and creates a feeling that summer is really here. However, if you ask people if they think robins are migratory, they will almost all answer in the negative. The robin may be the country's favourite but it is just not on the public's radar as a migrating bird.

We have seen in earlier chapters that there are always robins who do not follow the 'usual' rules. Excepting these birds, the general shape of migration is as follows.

The majority of birds that overwinter in the UK are dominant males with a well-defined territory. Whilst during the summer months their environment would support them, their partner and youngsters as they fledge, in the winter this changes and the males will aggressively drive out others and hold the space alone.

Therefore it can be said at its simplest level that migrating robins are mainly female, birds of both sexes in their first year or small weaker males without a territory. These migrants can find their way as far south as Algeria, with some stopping in France or Italy. The journey will be worth it for the food available in warmer places and during their stay, they will cut themselves territories as they would in Britain but they will not breed.

We have robins that migrate to us from even colder areas of northern Europe. A rise in birds successfully bred that year (more competition for territories) or a fail in the autumn berry crops may lead to an increase in the migration of European robins.

It is impossible to tell if the robin you see in your garden is a UK resident or visitor from somewhere colder, unless of course it has a particular marking or physical trait. There are slight differences; visitors are a little heavier, paler, with a slightly wider wing span and, above all, they are not quite as tame as the home-grown birds.

Migration is done at night, perhaps the safest time to travel if you are a small bird and, rather than taking the journey as one long effort like swallows, the robin will move from bush to bush, hedge to hedge, tree to tree with short bursts of longer flight between. Naturally, because we are an island, at some point they will

have to fly across water and there are well-documented instances of birds landing on boats in the Channel for a rest. The Channel Islands and other small offshore landfall can be a useful staging post too.

The majority of birds will overwinter in the UK, staying within several miles of the area in which they were fledged. However, migration is something that robins do both in and out of the country. This fact adds another layer to our fascination with the robin.

Tales from the Robin's Nest

Andrew Fusek Peters

When my chum the wonderful wildlife photographer, poet and writer Andrew Fusek Peters heard that my next book was to be *The Robin Book*, he sent me these terrific pictures and a little explanation to go with each set. What a lucky author I am to be able to include such brilliant images. The words and pictures are his, the delight is ours.

Tale 1

As we drew up our car and got out after a shopping trip, my son pointed his finger at the stone wall next to the car. 'Robin's nest!' he exclaimed, and there it was, near enough to reach out and touch, a delicate half bowl inside our hanging winter heather that had recently gone over. Incredible! My commute for wildlife photography from our house was precisely two yards!

Over the next week I followed its progress as the robin perched on our car aerial for worms, two close-ups to show chicks and surroundings in context.

The adults were not bothered by my interest, bringing endless feasts for their young ones, until one day as I watched with my long lens from the far side of the road, the chicks all tumbled out of the nest and began hopping up and down the lane. It seemed like a suicidal form of fledging as they were totally flightless but over the next few days I found no squashed robins so hope they made it into the air. It was amazing to see these hopping bundles of fluff! And I silently thanked the robins for feeling safe enough to choose our garden wall to bring new life into the world.

Tale 2

I first met Lynne at the cheese counter of the local farm shop. Because she had seen my pics in the papers, she was keen to tell me about the robin nesting in her shed. As I tasted a lovely mature Gruyère, she gave me her number and we arranged for me to come over.

A few days later, I was greeted by two huge and very soppy black labradors as I was led round the side of an old stone village house to a scruffy garden filled with unkempt grass and some hens that obviously ruled the roost. The shed she spoke of was an open-sided sagging wooden structure and with all the canine leaping about and chicken strutting, I was surprised any creature would want to take up residence. But this sums up the resilience of robin, a companionable bird who has evolved to live amongst us humans with barely a flighty worry in the world.

The nest itself was squeezed into a

corner among old ply, scaffolding tubes and industrial detritus. It was a little delicate construction of moss, with some old tape measure to tie it all together. The male was off and about to get food for the female, who sat on her chicks with protective grace. They ignored me totally and I was able to catch the incredible moment as the male brought in a jewelled cranefly. A few days later, the mother was seen shepherding her chicks around the garden and fledging was later successful. Fair play to the brave robins!

British Trust for
Ornithology

Looking out for birds

'Looking out for birds' is at the very heart of what the British Trust for Ornithology do. During the course of a year as many as 60,000 volunteers are out and about watching birds and submitting their observations, using structured scientific methods to do so. These data then allow BTO scientists to produce a variety of outputs that themselves contain interesting and inspiring stories. These outputs and results are published in scientific journals and the popular press, and form the backbone of important reports. They are the basis on which they produce their annual trends, which help keep an eye on the ups and downs of Britain's birds and other wildlife.

For example, during the last twenty-five years Britain has lost almost half of its breeding cuckoos (see page 97) and nearly all of its breeding turtle

doves (opposite). During the same period the great spotted woodpecker population has more than doubled and that of the robin has grown by 51%. Without this information it would be difficult to formulate meaningful conservation targets and actions.

Turtle dove

Barn owl

Cuckoo

Such surveys suit all levels of experience, from observing the birds in a person's garden for Garden BirdWatch, to recording all the birds people hear and see along a defined route for the BTO/ JNCC /RSPB Breeding Bird Survey. These surveys are often the first to highlight population changes, such as the huge decline in Britain's house sparrows which was first noticed in people's gardens.

But surveys aren't everything. Membership of the BTO also enables scientists to undertake research that other sources might not fund. By sponsoring BTO's work, members allow key projects to continue, such as pioneering work tracking cuckoos to Africa and back and revealing the conservation pinch-points for this iconic species in the process. In other words, there is a BTO for everyone. Find out more about BTO today by visiting www.bto.org.

The Robin in
Myth and Legend

The Robin in Myth and Legend

When I started researching this book I realised that everybody has a story about robins; they are very special to so many people. There was the woman cycling to work through the park, who was harangued by a robin in the middle of the path as she pondered whether to resign from her job or not. (She took the robin's advice and did.) Many people talk of seeing a robin when they visit a loved one's grave, being 'visited' by a robin on a loved one's anniversary or seeing a robin when feeling particularly depressed and needing a spiritual lift.

Wonderland by Kirsty Mitchell

The fine art photographer Kirsty Mitchell, whilst grieving at the death of her mother, took five years to create her highly acclaimed book *Wonderland* in her memory. In the book she describes how, on the last day of the whole shoot, in an isolated, snow-covered field, were the four who had started the whole project together five years earlier: Kirsty, her husband Matt, her assistant and the model. Kirsty had just started photographing the set-up, when suddenly and with snow falling, a robin arrived from nowhere. Having first landed on Kirsty's feet, it then went to the model in her enormously elaborate flower-covered costume and, whilst Kirsty was shooting, moved around the model's body. On the hand, on the arm, on the shoulders, on the head. Finally, after several minutes, the robin flew back to the three 'behind the camera' and after landing on the cover protecting Kirsty and her camera, it puffed up in front of Matt (who had been filming the whole incident on his phone) so that it and Kirsty were in the shot together. Then, as quickly as it had arrived, it disappeared. To see the little film of this amazing moment and to get a sense of the 'Wonderland' magic go to www.kirstymitchellphotography. com/portfolio/video-rough-behind-scenes-footage-making-home-wonderland-series/.

These personal stories are just that, personal, but there are also some well-documented myths and legends surrounding the robin. In defining a myth, Aristotle explained that, in the main, it has a basis in true and credible facts which have, over time and with the benefit of the oral tradition, been exaggerated somewhat. A house fairy in a time when such things were believed in (pre-Harry Potter) had the generic

name of Robin. Robin Goodfellow is one you might know from *A Midsummer Night's Dream*. It could be logically suggested that our human-loving, house-loving bird might be thought to bring good luck and therefore be a 'Robin'. This is an hypothesis with only slightly documented support but I offer it here to help as a link to the next thought concerning myth and legend: Christianity.

Christianity

It is not really understood why there seem to be so many legends in Christianity about the robin as there is no bird in the Middle East of this type. (Perhaps it was inspired by a distant pagan myth.) However, nativity tales include one in which the plain brown robin flies down from the rafters to fan the fire when the

stable seems too cold and, in doing so, scorches its breast. An Irish story from County Clare (*Spideog Mhuire* or *Mary's Robin*) has the robin following Mary when she and Joseph escape to Egypt with the babe. The robin covered her bloodied footprints so none could follow, but his chest was stained.

The crucifixion has two stories, one that the robin tried to remove thorns from the head of Christ and another that when the body was taken down from the cross, the robin covered it with leaves. Both legends are used to explain the red breast of the bird. Finally, the helpful and caring robin feels sorry for souls in hell and, on carrying water drops down to quench their thirst, has his chest singed.

Robin legends

There are two saints with robin legends too: St. Kentigern (also known as St. Mungo, Bishop of Glasgow, 516 AD) and St. Leonorius (570 AD).

As a child at a monastery school, St. Kentigern was a very clever and intelligent student, much loved by his teacher St. Serf (sometimes St. Servan) and much bullied by his classmates, who constantly tried to blame all problems on him. St. Serf had a pet robin and one day the bullies decided to kill the robin, pulling off its head and blaming the whole cruel event on Kentigern. However, when Kentigern held the feathered body and head in his hands, the legend tells that he prayed to heaven, set the head in line where it should be and the robin came back to life, flew to St. Serf's shoulder and sang for joy. This amazingly detailed building mural can be found in High Street, Glasgow, just beyond its junction with George Street and Duke Street. A contemporary work showing St. Mungo (Kentigern) and robins, it was created by the well-known Glasgow graffiti artist Sam Bates, a.k.a. Smug.

St. Leonorius went with other monks from Wales to found a monastery in Brittany. The legend has the monks preparing the soil for their first harvest, only to discover that they have brought no seeds to plant. However, while standing discussing what they should do, a robin alights nearby with a wheat-ear in its beak. (In an alternative version the robin leads the monks to a grain store.) Suffice to say the grain is planted and

an abundant harvest ensues. There is a special phrase in Brittany meaning "small beginnings that prosper" and it is "Robin Redbreast's Corn".

Irish legends

There are two Irish legends which have the robin (*spideóg*) gaining his red breast, firstly to help the other birds and secondly to help a father and son. One winter long ago, the

frost is hard and long and the birds gather to discuss what is to be done as they are slowly starving. The robin, back then a dull brown bird, has an idea and hurries off to a cottage where he can see a man clearing a path. Robin very bravely hops up to the man and stays close to him whilst he is sweeping. The man, realising the bird must be hungry to be so friendly, goes and gets a tray of crumbs for him. Robin flies off and gets the other birds to join in at the feast and through the hard season the birds are fed by this and the other households the robin had 'tamed' into providing food. The birds, in gratitude for their survival, made him a small red waistcoat, which he still wears.

The second Irish legend has a father and son finding themselves on a journey in open countryside when they need to stop as they are exhausted. The father builds a fire and he and the son agree to take it in turns to watch it so it will burn brightly and keep wolves away. When it is his turn, the son quickly falls asleep but a canny brown robin nearby realises that the wolves are circling so he fans the flames to keep the fire up and burning brightly, singeing his own breast in the process. The father and son survive and the robin gains his famous red breast.

First image of a robin in a religious text

Robin is sometimes used as a diminutive of the name Robert, and part of a fifteenth-century manuscript seems to contain the first use of an image of a robin in a religious text. Saint Robert of Bury

(St. Edmunds) died in 1181. The boy martyr's death was attributed to a blood libel perpetrated by local Jews on Good Friday. It would seem likely that the story was totally concocted to feed the rampant anti-semitism prevalent in this period. However, an image relating to the saint is held by the Fitzwilliam Museum in Cambridge; sadly it does not explain his martyrdom as there is no proper text and it was created some time after the original document to which it is attached. The picture shows a tonsured monk kneeling under a scroll on which, in Latin, are the words "Through the merits of St. Robert is offered here have compassion on me, and it for ever". The scroll leads up to a pair of hands holding a soul in a blanket or sheet. This image of the soul being lifted to heaven is also found on a seal of

The martyrdom of St. Robert of Bury, 1181.

Bury Abbey. There is a drape in front of the monk on which is a very clear depiction of a red-breasted bird.

*The Mausoleum Erected in Westminster Abbey, at the
Funeral Obsequies of* QUEEN MARY II.

Queen Mary II

In 1695, when Queen Mary II lay in state in Westminster Abbey, a robin came into the Abbey and spent several days sitting in the coffin area, singing and ultimately causing a sensation. There were many reports in the press and it became known as The Westminster Wonder. Here are some extracts from the transcript of a very long ballad sung to a well-known tune of the day, *The Jealous Lover*.

The Westminster Wonder;

Giving an Account of a Robin-Red-Breast, who, ever since the Queens Funeral continues on the Top Pinacle of the Queens Mausoleum or Pyramid, in the Abby of Westminster, where he is seen and heard to Sing, and will not depart the Place, to the Admiration of many Beholders.

This is a Wonder strange, I say,
Ere since that great and solemn Day,
Of the Interment of our Queen,
There is a Robin Red-Brest seen,

Upon the very Top of all:
He sings a Note soft, sweet, and small,
Which is most pleasant for to hear,
When they the Royal Place draw near.

Sometimes it flies a little way,
Yet from the Place it will not stay,
But soon returns with speed again,
Where it doth Night and Day remain.

Upon the pinacle it sits
Spreading its little Wings by fits,
And in the very midst of Prayer,
This Robin he sits singing there,

[...]

Renowned Lords and Ladies gay,
And common People day by day,
Upon their hearing this Report,
They to the Abby all resort,

Where Robin Red-breast they behold,
Upon the pinacle of Gold;
And it's the Thoughts of Rich
and Poor,
The like was never known before.

[...]

'Robin' the postman

The robin was originally known to all as the ruddock, derived from the Anglo-Saxon *run*, meaning red, and we gained the term ruddy from this source too. However, the bird actually came to be known nationally as the robin through the British postal service. In 1793 the first postman's uniform was issued in London and it was a scarlet tailcoat with lapels and cuffs in blue. These very visible postal workers were nicknamed robins or redbreasts and so, as would seem logical, the name robin stuck to the bird with the red breast. Although by 1837 the postman's jacket was blue, there was still a scarlet collar and gradually, through the Victorian period, the uniform was taken on across the nation and the nickname spread too. That well-known former employee of the Post Office Anthony Trollope describes a scene in his 1861 novel *Framley Parsonage* thus: *"'Oh, but it's mortial wet,' said the shivering postman as he handed in that and the vicar's newspaper. The vicar was a man of the world, and took the Jupiter.*

'Come in, Robin postman, and warm theeself awhile,' said Jemima the cook, pushing a stool a little to one side, but still well in front of the big kitchen fire."

Christmas card

The first Christmas card was sent in 1843 by Henry Cole, postal reformer

and Director of the Victoria & Albert Museum. Previously there had been a British tradition of sending cards at New Year but Cole had helped inaugurate the penny post and suddenly more people were sending greetings. He therefore decided to devise something special to communicate with his family and friends at a time when he was at his busiest. He got his friend and artist John Callcott Horsley to design something for him and although initially slow to catch on, within twenty years the custom of sending mass-produced cards was firmly established. Until the turn of the century, the post was still delivered on Christmas Day, so 'robin' the postman was often depicted on cards as 'robin' the bird, delivering Christmas post. Early cards were not religious and gradually the robin (the bird) became synonymous with Christmas.

Superstitions

You might expect, with a bird so connected to humans, that there would be many superstitions associated with the robin... and you would be correct. They are rather good weather indicators; a robin singing in the open means good weather on its way, whilst singing in the bushes means it will rain. Harming a robin, its nest, its eggs or its young was considered very unlucky in times past. A folk rhyme states, "The blood on the breast of a robin that's caught, brings death to the snarer by whom it is caught." Your deeds would find you out. Some areas of the country went further and believed if a nest pillager broke the bird's wing or leg, they too would suffer a broken arm or leg. A robin in the house meant someone who lived there would die and a robin in a church meant a congregation member would die. The ultimate indicator of the end of life was to have a robin tap on the window of a sick person calling 'weep, weep'. However, there is a cheery superstition too, that if a robin is the first bird you see on St. Valentines day, hang out the flags, you'll marry a sailor!

The Robin in
Art and Literature

The Robin in Art and Literature

There is one outstanding thing about robins – the red breast – but as you will know from the photographs in this book, in actual fact a robin's chest feathers are orange. However, the English language did not gain the word for orange (named for the fruit) until the sixteenth century, and so it was referred to as red and that is the word that stuck. The robin orange-breast does not have quite the same ring about it.

One of the first mentions of a robin proper comes in Geoffrey Chaucer's *Parlement of Foules* (1381-1382). In the central section of the 699 lines, Chaucer gives each bird its category. In line 345, *"The theef, the chough and eek the jangling pie"*, he is describing

a member of the crow family as a thief and a magpie as having a rattling call. Later, in line 349, we meet *"The tame rodok and the coward kite"*, the robin having first been known as a ruddock.

I have discussed in the Myths and Legends chapter the idea of robins being associated with death; covering the dead with moss or leaves, caring for the spirit of the dead and even offering solace to those left behind. Perhaps the first appearance in literature of this idea was the publication of an anonymous broadside ballad in Norwich in 1595. The title, "The Norfolk gent his will and Testament and howe he Commytted the keepinge of his Children to his own brother whoe delte most wickedly with them and howe God plagued him for it",

makes it very clear what happened. The origin of the story is said to be Wayland Wood in Norfolk, with the uncle living at Griston Hall, quite close to the wood. To this day the wood is said to be haunted by the children and the village of Griston acknowledges the story on its village sign.

In its simplest form the story tells of two small children who are orphaned and are taken to live with their uncle until they attain their majority. All the money from their parents is left to them, unless they die, in which case the residual legatee is the uncle. Perhaps not surprisingly he decides to kill them, but being unable to do the deed himself, he sends the children with two henchmen into the nearby wood.

He bargained with two ruffians strong,
Who were of furious mood,
That they should take these children young
And slaye thim in a wood.

One of the assassins takes pity on the children, kills the other assassin and abandons them in the wood to their fate. The robin features in the original text as at the end it reads:

In one another's arms they died
awanting due relief:
No burieal this pretty pair
Of any man receives,
Till Robin redbreast piously
Did cover them with leaves

This particular narrative has been reworked many times and in several forms since then. Perhaps the clearest explanation is an illustrated book by Randolph Caldecott, published in 1879. The words of the anonymous poem most often quoted about this story fill in the rest of the sorry tale.

The robins start to cover the babes, illustration by Randolph Caldecott.

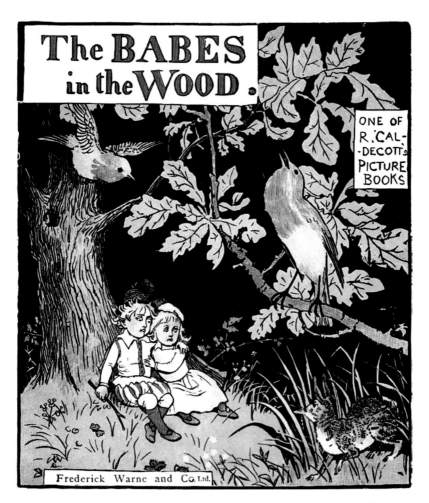

The BABES in the WOOD.

ONE OF R. CAL-
-DECOTT's PICTURE
BOOKS

Frederick Warne and Co. Ltd.

My dear, do you know how, a long time ago,
Two poor little children, whose names I don't know,
Were stolen away on a bright summer day
And left in the woods, so I've heard people say.

And when it was night, how sad was their plight.
The sun, it went down, and the moon gave no light.
They sobbed and they sighed, and they bitterly cried,
'Til the poor little things, they lay down and died.

And when they were dead, the robin so red
Brought strawberry leaves and over them spread,
And all the day long, he sang this sad song:
"Poor babes in the wood, poor babes in the wood."
And don't you remember the babes in the wood.

Anonymous

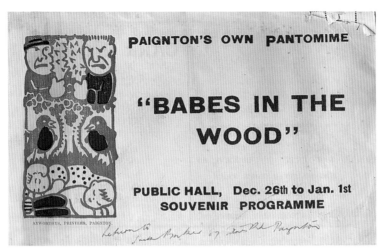

PAIGNTON'S OWN PANTOMIME

"BABES IN THE WOOD"

PUBLIC HALL, Dec. 26th to Jan. 1st
SOUVENIR PROGRAMME

AXWORTHYS, PRINTERS, PAIGNTON.

Programme for the 1935 production at Paignton in Devon.

At the other end of the dramatic scale, but still using the same story is *Babes in the Wood* the pantomime. This is perhaps the only occasion in which a robin is acknowledged as part of the plot. Here the uncle of the Griston account is most often named as the 'Wicked Baron', the murderers are 'Good and Bad Robbers' but the leaving of the children and the covering with leaves is still there.

It was first produced at Drury Lane in 1827 under the title 'Harlequin and Cock Robin: or The Babes in the Wood'. Unlike the poem and the original 1595 version, the scene in the wood and the covering with leaves is traditionally at the end of Act One in the pantomime, leaving plenty of space for the 'development' and, as you would expect, there is of course a happy ending.

Victorian productions might even feature a female chorus 'flying' in as the birds. These days, cost being king, lighting and stage tricks create the atmosphere for fewer birds. Strangely, you may also find versions of this performance which include, rather oddly, Robin Hood and his entourage, the two stories being joined by the notion that the babes are found in Sherwood Forest.

There are many inclusions of robins in prose, poems and songs through the centuries. Whole books have been written just about the art and literature. I hope you will accept these listed here as just a taster of the many out there, should you care to go searching.

In Shakespeare's *Cymbeline*, a quote spoken over the body of Imogen states:

I'll sweeten thy sad grave;
Thou shalt not lack
The flowers that's like thy face,
pale primrose, nor
The azur'd harebell...
The ruddock would
With charitable bill bring thee all this
Yea, and furr'd moss besides, when flowers are none,
To winter-ground thy corse.

Cornelia, on finding her son is dead in John Webster's play *The White Devil* (1612) explains how her grandmother would sing a lament on the death of a family member:

Call for the Robin Redbreast and the Wren,
Since o'er shady groves they hover,
And with leaves and flowers do cover
The friendless bodies of unburied men.

Who kill'd Cock Robin?
  I, said the Sparrow,
    With my bow and arrow,
And I kill'd Cock Robin.

This is the Sparrow,
With his bow and arrow. (1)

Who caught his blood?
  I, said the Fish,
    With my little dish,
And I caught his blood.

This is the Fish
That held the dish. (2)

The famous nursery rhyme of 1744 'Who Killed Cock Robin' has since become a hook on which to hang many tales, dramas and detective stories. (N.B. it is generally understood that the bell-ringing 'bull' was a bullfinch and therefore another bird, rather than a bovine.)

Who killed Cock Robin?
– Anon

Who killed Cock Robin?
I, said the Sparrow,
with my bow and arrow,
I killed Cock Robin.

Who saw him die?
I, said the Fly,
with my little eye,
I saw him die.

Who caught his blood?
I, said the Fish,
with my little dish,
I caught his blood.

Who'll make the shroud?
I, said the Beetle,
with my thread and needle,
I'll make the shroud.

Who'll dig his grave?
I, said the Owl,
with my little trowel,
I'll dig his grave.

Who'll be the parson?
I, said the Rook,
with my little book,
I'll be the parson.

Who'll be the clerk?
I, said the Lark,
if it's not in the dark,
I'll be the clerk.

Who'll carry the link?
I, said the Linnet,
I'll fetch it in a minute,
I'll carry the link.

In 1861, taxidermist Walter Potter staged the *Death of
Cock Robin* with 98 different species of embalmed birds.

Who'll be chief mourner?
I, said the Dove,
I mourn for my love,
I'll be chief mourner.

Who'll carry the coffin?
I, said the Kite,
if it's not through the night,
I'll carry the coffin.

Who'll bear the pall?
We, said the Wren,
both the cock and the hen,
We'll bear the pall.

Who'll sing a psalm?
I, said the Thrush,
as she sat on a bush,
I'll sing a psalm.

Who'll toll the bell?
I, said the Bull,
because I can pull,
I'll toll the bell.

All the birds of the air
fell a-sighing and a-sobbing,
when they heard the bell toll
for poor Cock Robin.

Death and Burial of Poor Cock Robin by H. L. Stephens, 1865.

John Clare (1793-1864)

Of all English writers of nature poetry, I would suggest that one of the greatest is John Clare (1793-1864). If you are unfamiliar with his history and work, do look him up, you will not be disappointed. His output was enormous and happily underwent something of a renaissance during the late twentieth century. By nature of his actually being a farm labourer and son of the soil, the quality and insightfulness of his poetry shines through. He has much to say about the robin and rather than put several poems here, I have put in the whole of *The Autumn Robin*, his longest on the subject. Often scratching around for anything to write on, his was the ultimate struggle for his art. He had mental health problems in later life and was confined in an asylum twice before finally dying there in 1864.

John Clare by William Hilton, 1820.

His tombstone reads:

To the Memory of John Clare The
Northamptonshire Peasant Poet.
A Poet is Born not Made.

The Autumn Robin by John Clare (1820)

Sweet little Bird in russet coat,
 The livery of the closing year1
I love thy lonely plaintive note,
 And tiney whispering song to hear.
While on the stile or garden seat,
 I sit to watch the falling leaves,
Thy songs thy little joys repeat,
 My loneliness relieves.

And many are the lonely minds
 That hear, and welcome thee anew;
Not taste alone, but humble hinds,
 Delight to praise and love thee too.
The veriest clown, beside his cart,
 Turns from his song with many a smile,
To see thee from the hedgrow start,
 And sing upon the stile.

The shepherd on the fallen tree
 Drops down to listen to thy lay,
And chides his dog beside his knee,
 Who barks, and frightens thee away.
The hedger pauses ere he knocks
 The stake down in the meadow gap -
The Boy who every songster mocks,
 Forbears the gate to clap.

When in the hedge that hides the post
 Thy ruddy bosom he surveys -
Pleased with thy song, in pleasure lost,
 He pauses mutters scraps of praise.
The maiden marks, at days decline,
 Thee in the yard, on broken plough,
And stops her song, to listen thine,
 While milking brindled cow.

Thy simple faith in man's esteem,
 From every heart hath favours won;
Dangers to thee no dangers seem -
 Thou seemest to court them more then shun.
The clown in winter takes his gun,
 The barn door flocking birds to slay,
Yet shouldst thou in the danger run
 He turns the tube away.

John Clare Memorial, Helpston, Cambridgeshire.

The gipsy boy, who seeks in glee
  Blackberrys for a dainty meal,
Laughs loud on first beholding thee,
  When called, so near his presence
steal.
For sure he thinks thou knew'st the call;
  And tho his hunger ill can spare
The fruit, he will not pluck them all,
  But leaves some to thy share.

Up on the ditcher's spade thou'lt hop,
  For grubs and wreathing worms to
search;
Where woodmen in the forest chop,
  Thou'lt fearless on their faggots perch;
Nay, by the gipies' camp I stop,
  And mark thee perch a moment there,
To prune thy wing awhile, then drop,
  The littered crumbs to share.

Domestic bird! thy pleasant face
  Doth well thy common suit commend;
To meet thee in a stranger-place
  Is meeting with an ancient friend.

I track the thicket's glooms around,
  And there, as loath to leave, again
Thou comest, as if thou knew the sound
  And loved the sight of men.

The lonliest wood that man can trace
  To thee a pleasant dwelling gives;
In every town and crowded place
  The sweet domestic robin lives.
Go where we will, in every spot
  Thy little welcome mates appear;
And like the daisy's common lot,
  Thou'rt met with every where.

The swallow in the chimney tier,
  The tittering martin in the eaves,
With half of love and half of fear
  Their mortared dwelling shily weaves;
The sparrows in the thatch will shield;
  Yet they, as well as e'er they can,
Contrive with doubtful faith to build
  Beyond the reach of man.

But thou'rt less timid then the wren,
  Domestic and confiding bird!

And spots, the nearest haunts of men,
  Are oftenest for thy home preferred.
In garden-walls thou'lt build so low,
  Close where the bunch of fennel stands,
That e'en a child just learned to go
  May reach with tiny hands.

Sweet favoured bird! thy under notes
  In summers music grows unknown,
The concert from a thousand throats
  Leaves thee as if to pipe alone;
No listening ear the shepherd lends,
  The simple ploughman marks thee not,
And then by all thy autumn friends
  Thou'rt missing and forgot.

The far-famed nightingale, that shares
  Cold public praise from every tongue,
The popular voice of music heirs,
  And injures much thy under-song.
Yet then my walks thy theme salutes;
  And finds their autumn's favoured
guest,

Gay piping on the hazel-roots
  Above thy mossy nest.

'Tis wrong that thou shouldst be
despised,
  When these gay fickle birds appear;
They sing when summer flowers are
prized -
  Thou at the dull and dying year.
Well! let the heedless and the gay
  Bepraise the voice of louder lays,
The joy thou steal'st from Sorrow's day
  Is more to thee then praise.

And could my notes steal aught from
thine,
  My words but imitate thy lay,
Time would not then his charge resign,
  Nor throw the meanest verse away,
But ever at this mellow time,
  He should thine Autumn praise prolong,
As they would share the happy prime
  Of thy eternal song.

The Redbreast Chasing the Butterfly by William Wordsworth (1815)

In this first verse from the poem *The Redbreast Chasing the Butterfly* (1815), William Wordsworth starts by acknowledging how beloved the bird is in our heritage:

Art thou the bird whom Man loves best,
The pious bird with the scarlet breast,
    Our little English Robin;
The bird that comes about our doors
When Autumn-winds are sobbing?
Art thou the Peter of Norway Boors?
    Their Thomas in Finland,
    And Russia far inland?
The bird, that by some name or other
All men who know thee call their
brother,
The darling of children and men?
Could Father Adam open his eyes
And see this sight beneath the skies,
He'd wish to close them again.

Portrait of William Wordsworth by William Shuter, 1798.

Beatrix Potter

In 1902 Beatrix Potter commercially published her first book, *The Tale of Peter Rabbit*. (Initially she had printed it privately in black and white in 1901. This was the first commercial printing in full colour, which publishers Fredrick Warne and Co. had always wanted from their first sight of the manuscript.) Although Potter never wrote specifically about

robins, as a keen gardener and farmer she obviously understood their relationship with man. In perhaps one of her most iconic Peter Rabbit illustrations, Peter is seen chomping through Mr. McGregor's carrots and he is being applauded in song by a robin on the handle of a garden fork.

The Secret Garden by Francis Hodgeson Burnett (1911)

Another book from children's literature in which the robin features as a central character is *The Secret Garden* by Francis Hodgeson Burnett (1911). Burnett had a very personal relationship with robins, writing a book, *My Robin* in 1912, describing her relationship with a robin in her garden. Although born in Manchester in 1849, she moved to the United States when she was sixteen but

American robin.

came back to spend many years in the UK before finally returning to the US permanently in 1907. It is important to note that when she speaks of a robin she means a UK robin and not the altogether larger US robin. That bird is about the size of a thrush and has none of the characteristics of its namesake from England.

When asked at the beginning of *My Robin* if she owned it, she writes: "I did not own the robin—he owned

The original cover of *The Secret Garden*, 1911 by
M. L. Kirk.

me—or perhaps we owned each
other. He was an English robin and
he was a PERSON—not a mere
bird. An English robin differs greatly
from the American one. He is much
smaller and quite differently shaped.
His body is daintily round and plump,
his legs are delicately slender.
He is a graceful little patrician
with an astonishing allurement of
bearing. His eye is large and dark
and dewy; he wears a tight little red
satin waistcoat on his full round
breast and every tilt of his head,
every flirt of his wing is instinct
with dramatic significance. He is
fascinatingly conceited—he burns
with curiosity—he is determined to
engage in social relations at almost
any cost and his raging jealousy of
attention paid to less worthy objects
than himself drives him at times to
efforts to charm and distract which
are irresistible. An intimacy with a
robin—an English robin—is a liberal

education." This description exactly sums up the relationship of the robin to man.

The next paragraph to quote from *My Robin* is an insight into how Francis Hodgeson Burnett came to find the words to describe the child/bird meeting in *The Secret Garden*:

"Without stirring a muscle I began to make low, soft, little sounds to him—very low and very caressing indeed—softer than one makes to a baby. I wanted to weave a spell—to establish mental communication—to make Magic. And as I uttered the tiny sounds he hopped nearer and nearer.

'Oh! to think that you will come as near as that!' I whispered to him. 'You KNOW. You know that nothing in the world would make me put out my hand or startle you in the least tiniest way. You know it because you are a real person as well as a lovely—lovely little bird thing. You know it because

Mary finds the door to the garden in the 1912 illustration by Charles Robinson.

you are a soul.' Because of this first morning I knew—years later—that this was what Mistress Mary thought when she bent down in the Long Walk and 'tried to make robin sounds.'"

The central character of *The Secret Garden* is a lonely, sad ten-year-old called Mary Lennox. Born and brought up in India, not by her parents, who did not love her, but by Indian 'staff' who adhered to her every whim, she has no idea how the world really turns. When her parents and Indian nanny all die in a cholera epidemic, she is sent back to England to live in a barely inhabited mansion on the Yorkshire moors.

The Secret Garden describes her slow understanding of the nature of 'nature' and also of love. The robin shows Mary how to get into the garden of the title which, like her, has been untouched and unloved for ten years. Mary connects with a garden boy from the moors called Dickon, who eventually helps her bring the garden back to life. The garden is not just good for Mary of course but also her bedridden cousin Colin, who she discovers shut away in a corner of Misselthwaite Manor. With the help of Dickon and the robin, both the children come back to life and love through an understanding of how nature works. Whilst initially written for children, it has much to offer adults and if you don't know it, it is well worth searching out. (Do read it before you see any film adaptations, there are several good ones but the book has the quality of the tale – the pictures from words are so much better in books than on film!)

The Robin by Thomas Hardy (1840-1928)

When up aloft
I fly and fly,
I see in pools
The shining sky,
And a happy bird
Am I, am I!

When I descend
Towards their brink
I stand, and look,
And stoop, and drink,
And bathe my wings,
And chink and prink.

When winter frost
Makes earth as steel
I search and search
But find no meal,
And most unhappy
Then I feel.

But when it lasts,
And snows still fall,
I get to feel
No grief at all,
For I turn to a cold stiff
Feathery ball!

The Redbreast by Anthony Rye from The Inn of the Birds (1947)

The redbreast smoulders in the waste of snow:
His eye is large and bright, and to and fro
He draws and draws his slender threads of sound
Between the dark boughs and the freezing ground.

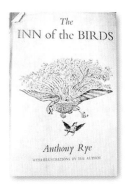

The Inn of the Birds was written and illustrated by Rye, who was an illustrator and engraver as well as a poet. From the 1940s he lived in Selbourne, a village famous through the work of Gilbert White, for its connection to nature.

Rodney Bennett (1890-1948) wrote children's books and poetry and is the father of the much more famous composer Sir Richard Rodney Bennett.

Robin's Song by Rodney Bennett

Robins sang in England,
Frost or rain or snow,
All the long December days
Endless years ago.
Robins sang in England
Before the Legions came,
Before our English fields were tilled
Or England was a name.
Robins sang in England
When forests dark and wild
Stretched across from sea to sea
And Jesus was a child.
Listen! in the frosty dawn
From his leafless bough
The same brave song he ever sang
A robin's singing now.

The Robin Book

Round Robin by Dru Marland

Not slim

And far from win-

some, the round robin sings

In unmelodious tones of things familial;

Who passed what exam, did well at work, had chil-

dren of rare beauty; feathers puffed with pride; but still

Behind the seming gasconading, someone strove

To keep the distant bonds, with time worn thin,

In place, that complicated love

That families have

Within.

Left: Image by Dru Marland to accompany the poem.

Robin's Round
by U. A. Fanthorpe

I am the proper
Bird for this season –
Not blessed St Turkey,
Born to be eaten.
I'm man's inedible
Permanent bird.
I dine in his garden,
My spoon is his spade.
I'm the true token
Of Christ the Child-King:
I nest in man's stable,
I eat at man's table,
Through all his dark winters
I sing.

With kind permission of the estate of
U. A. Fanthorpe and Enitharmon Editions
www.enitharmon.co.uk

Pairings by Deborah Harvey

That April
back when I'd still make tea for two
though only one was needed

I'd sit at the table, watch the birds –
thrushes, wrens, the pair of robins
perched on the bird bath,

glad they'd made it through the winter,
that the male was courting his mate
with juicy wrigglers.

You're here now
but I'm distractible,
it's you who brews the tea

and as often as not
I let it grow cold
yet in the moment of its bringing

I'll open my beak, quiver my wings
as if I might still sing the quickening
song of springtime.

Robin
Anonymous

Robin sang sweetly
When the days were bright.
'Thanks, thanks for summer,'
He sang with all his might.

Robin sang sweetly,
In the autumn days,
'There are fruits for everyone,
Let all give praise.'

In the cold and wintry weather,
Sill hear his song:
'Somebody must sing,' said Robin
'Or winter will seem long.'

When the spring came back again
He sang, 'I told you so!
Keep on singing through the winter
It will always go.'

An Epitaph on a Robin-Redbreast
by Samuel Rogers

Tread lightly here, for here, 'tis said,
When piping winds are hush'd around,
A small note wakes from underground,
Where now his tiny bones are laid.

No more in lone and leafless groves,
With ruffled wing and faded breast,
His friendless, homeless spirit roves;
Gone to the world where birds are blest!

Where never cat glides o'er the green,
Or school-boy's giant form is seen;
But Love, and Joy, and smiling Spring
Inspire their little souls to sing!

The Little Robin Grieves
Anonymous

The little robin grieves
When the snow is on the ground,
For the trees have no leaves,
And no berries can be found.

The air is cold, the worms are hid:
For robin here what can be done?
Let's strow around some crumbs
of bread,
And then he'll live till snow is gone.

The Secret
Anonymous

We have a secret, just we three,
The robin, and I, and the sweet cherry-tree;
The bird told the tree, and the tree told me,
And nobody knows it but just us three.

But of course the robin knows it best,
Because she built the—I shan't tell the rest;
And laid the four little—something in it—
I'm afraid I shall tell it every minute.

But if the tree and the robin don't peep,
I'll try my best the secret to keep;
Though I know when the little birds fly about
Then the whole secret will be out.

Photo credits and artworks

The Robin in Art and Literature 114-155

Page 114: **'Solstice Song' by Catherine Hyde. www.catherinehyde.co.uk**

Page 116: Evelyn Simak

Page 118: Copyright free

Page 119: Copyright free

Page 120: Copyright free

Page 122: Paignton Panto Productions

Page 124: Public domain review

Page 126: Public domain review

Page 127: Copyright free

Page 128: Public domain

Page 130: Rodney Burton

Page 133: Public domain

Page 134: Wikipedia

Page 135: Robert Nunnally

Page 136: Copyright free

Page 137: Public domain

Page 139: **'Robin in Spring Garden' by Dru Marland.**

Page 141: **'Robin' by Karin Celestine. www.celestineandthehare.com**

Page 142: Robin Morrison (right)

Page 143: **Illustration and wood burnings on birchwood by Jenny Steer. www.jennysteer.com**

Page 144: **'Round Robin for Poem' by Dru Marland.**

Page 146: **Robin by Tom Charlesworth. tomcharlesworthillustration.co.uk**

Page 149: **'Find the Robin' stained glass panel by Tamsin Abbott. www.tamsinabbott.co.uk**

Page 151: **'Robin' by Kate Wyatt. wwwkatewyattartist.co.uk**

Page 152: **'The Rising Moon' by Hannah Willow. www.hannahwillow.com**

Page 155: Grace's Guide to British Industrial History

Every effort has been made to trace copyright holders of material and acknowledge permission for this publication. The publisher apologises for any errors or omissions to rights holders and would be grateful for notification of credits and corrections that should be included in future reprints or editions of this book.

Acknowledgements

The superb photographers who have yet again come forward to help me with this book deserve even more applause than usual. When I originally put a call out for anyone with robin images, they responded in volume. However, what I had not allowed for was the posing nature of the robin.

Almost all of the submitted pics were great individually but definitely of the 'close-up robin looking left, looking right, looking straight ahead' type. Of course there were exceptions to this but they were thin on the ground and I was stumped. What was to be done? Fearing I might be told to get lost, I went back to them all and asked if they had pictures of robins that were more unusual. They rose to the challenge brilliantly and not one told me to take a hike. I am sure you will agree that they succeeded. Take a bow all you photographers...you deserve it!

My chum Mary Pyne deserves the heartiest of thank you acknowledgements. During a particularly hard section, she sent me a message almost every day with a motivational quote and an admonition to 'get on with it'. She also stepped up and did a basic read through for me, which elicited much laughter about our different attitudes to grammar! Thank you Mary, your support was invaluable.

The Robin Book
Published in Great Britain in 2019 by
Graffeg Limited

Written by Jane Russ copyright © 2019.
Designed and produced by Graffeg
Limited copyright © 2019

Graffeg Limited, 24 Stradey Park
Business Centre, Mwrwg Road,
Llangennech, Llanelli, Carmarthenshire
SA14 8YP Wales UK Tel 01554 824000
www.graffeg.com

ISBN 9781912654994

1 2 3 4 5 6 7 8 9